The Ultimate Egg

Cookbook

Omelets & Beyond – Super Tasty Ways to Cook an Egg

by - Joris Birt

....

Licensing Notice

• •

Table of Contents

Introduction

In a world where culinary possibilities seem endless, there is one humble ingredient that has stood the test of time and continues to amaze us with its versatility and deliciousness – the egg. Whether you're a seasoned chef, a home cook, or just someone who enjoys a hearty meal, eggs have undoubtedly found a permanent place in your kitchen. But have you ever stopped to truly appreciate the wonders that these oval-shaped treasures hold?

Imagine standing in front of your refrigerator, wondering what delightful dish to whip up for your next meal. You may have experienced that familiar feeling of indecision, settling for the same old recipes that have lost their charm over time. Fear not, for we have the perfect solution – eggs! While eggs have long been a staple in households worldwide, their limitless culinary possibilities often remain untapped. It's time to break away from the monotony and embrace the eggstravaganza of flavors and textures that lie ahead.

Within these pages, you will discover the hidden potential of eggs, as they lend their velvety textures and delightful flavors to an array of recipes that will leave you yearning for more.

Prepare to unlock the full potential of eggs, redefining what's possible in the kitchen and turning every meal into a work of art.

Tips and Tricks

Eggs are a versatile and nutritious staple in many households, offering an array of culinary possibilities. Whether you're a seasoned chef or a home cook, these valuable tips will ensure your egg dishes turn out just the way you desire.

1. Opt for Organic: Health-conscious individuals should consider choosing organic eggs for their superior quality and nutritional benefits.
2. Perfectly Hard-Boiled: Achieve the ideal hard-boiled egg by placing them in boiling water for approximately 10 minutes.
3. Delicate Soft-Boiled Eggs: For a runny or barely set yolk, gently simmer the eggs covered for 5-7 minutes before serving.
4. Fluffy Scrambled Eggs: To obtain a fluffy texture, add a few tablespoons of milk or mayonnaise and gently beat the eggs while tilting the bowl to incorporate air bubbles.
5. Mastering Omelets: Cook the egg base fully before adding fillings, then gently fold the omelet in half for a delightful result.
6. Poaching Perfection: Poach eggs in water to achieve a solidified white and a deliciously runny yolk.
7. Testing Freshness: Check an egg's freshness by placing it in a bowl of water; if it stays at the bottom on its side, it's fresh; if it floats, it's no longer suitable for consumption.
8. Egg Cups with a Twist: Elevate your egg cups by incorporating sliced vegetables like onions and bell peppers.
9. Buying Tips: Look for clean eggs free from cracks when purchasing to ensure quality.

10. Smart Storage: Keep eggs in their original packaging, stored on the coldest part of the refrigerator. Fresh eggs can last 3-5 weeks, while cooked leftovers should be consumed within 3 days.

11. Healthier Substitutions: Reduce calories, fat, and cholesterol by using egg whites as a substitute for half of the eggs in your recipes (2 egg whites = 1 whole egg).

By following these practical guidelines, you can elevate your egg-cooking skills and enjoy delightful, nutritious dishes for yourself and your family.

1. Classic Deviled Eggs

Nothing beats a classic. This recipe has been a hit on the appetizer list for ages. Whether served immediately or chilled until ready to enjoy, these deviled eggs are an irresistible classic that continues to be a hit at any gathering.

Serving Size: 12

Preparation Time: 15 minutes

Ingredients:

- 24 large eggs, hard-boiled, peeled, and halved
- 1/3 cup mayonnaise
- 1/3 cup sour cream
- 2 teaspoons lemon juice
- 1 ½ teaspoons Tabasco Sauce
- ½ teaspoon garlic powder
- 1 ½ tablespoons chopped parsley
- 1 ½ tablespoons fresh chopped tarragon
- 24 sprigs of tarragon for garnish
- 2 teaspoons salt
- 2 teaspoons black pepper
- 2 teaspoons paprika
- ¼ cup green onion, cut into slant strips

Instructions:

Scoop out the yolk of the eggs into a medium bowl and mix well with all the ingredients except for your egg whites, green onion, and paprika.

Pipe about a tablespoon of your yolk mixture into each egg white half then sprinkle with paprika and top with green onion slants.

Serve immediately or refrigerate 'til you are ready to serve.

2. Bacon-Lined Egg Cups

This recipe uses two all-time favorite ingredients - bacon and eggs. The sweet, salty taste of the bacon and the creamy, velvety taste of eggs is an all-time star. Instead of having regular muffins let's get creative and line those muffin tins with bacon, fill it with eggs and bake your perfect cups.

Serving Size: 6

Preparation Time: 30 minutes

Ingredients:

- 12 eggs
- 12 slices of bacon
- 1 ounce of cheese
- Salt and pepper

Instructions:

Heat oven to 350 degrees Fahrenheit.

Grease muffin tin with some non-stick spray.

Line muffin molds by pressing a bacon slice to the sides of each, be careful not to press slices to the bottom of the molds.

In each hole, cautiously break an egg. Add salt and pepper to taste.

Sprinkle cheese (optional).

Bake for 20 minutes or up to desired readiness.

3. Fluffy Egg White Muffins

These delicate, delicious, nutritious and healthy muffins are low in calories and low in fat and for extra nutritional value they are packed with lots of vegetables.

Serving Size: 12

Preparation Time: 50 minutes

Ingredients:

- 11 egg whites
- 2 cups of spinach
- 1 cup of corn
- 1 cup of chopped squash
- 1 onion, sliced
- 1 red pepper, chopped
- 1 tablespoon of olive oil
- 3 tablespoons of Mexican cheese
- 1 tablespoon of cumin
- 1 tablespoon of chili powder
- 1 tablespoon of fresh cilantro

Instructions:

Heat oven to 350 degrees

Chop vegetables and slice them into tiny chunks.

Warm olive oil over medium heat in your skillet over medium heat. Add onions and red peppers and sauté until onions are translucent. Toss in the corn and squash then add the spinach and toss 'til it is wilted, then add the spices. Mix in Mexican cheese until combined.

In your mixing bowl beat egg whites and vegetables together. Put aside.

Grease muffin tins lightly, then pour in egg and mixture of vegetables.

Bake for 25 minutes or until they are fluffy and fully cooked. Serve.

4. Scotch Eggs

This is an amazing dish and will enhance your taste buds. Made from hard-boiled eggs packed in layers of seasoned sausage meat, covered in crispy batter and then deep fried to a rich golden color. Perfect start to a great day!

Serving Size: 5

Preparation Time: 10 minutes

Ingredients:

- 2 cups good quality sausage meat
- 2 tablespoons chives, finely chopped
- 2 tablespoons parsley, finely chopped
- ½ tablespoon mustard
- ¼ cup and 1 tablespoon panko bread crumbs
- 1 quart vegetable oil (for frying)
- 2 tablespoons vegetable oil (for cooking)
- 5 hard-boiled eggs, peeled
- 2 eggs, beaten
- 1 cup flour
- Salt and pepper to taste

Instructions:

In your bowl, mix together the sausage meat, mustard, parsley, chives, salt and pepper. Mix well. Divide mixture in 5 balls.

Arrange 3 plates- first plate with flour, next plate with the beaten eggs, and last plate with the breadcrumbs.

Flatten the sausage balls and make it oval.

Then roll an egg into the flour, then cover the egg evenly with the meat mixture.

Dip the meat covered egg into the beaten eggs, then to the breadcrumbs. Do the same for the remaining eggs

In your frying pan, heat the vegetable oil until it sizzles. Fry the eggs until the breadcrumbs turn crispy and golden. Drain excess oil on some paper towel, and then serve.

5. Eggs and Bacon Quesadillas

Have yourself this protein packed, spicy, brunch to go. This is an incredibly quick, delicious, authentic Mexican flavored quesadilla, well put together with squishy cheese, rich and creamy eggs and the juiciest tomato salsa.

Serving Size: 1

Preparation Time: 20 minutes

Ingredients:

- ¼ cup store-bought Mexican blend shredded cheese (if not available, use 2 tablespoons shredded Monterey jack cheese + 2 tablespoons shredded sharp cheddar cheese)
- 1 flour tortilla
- 2 slices of Canadian style bacon
- 2 eggs, beaten
- ½ cup store-bought tomato salsa

Instructions:

Sprinkle 2 tbsp of Mexican blend cheese over the tortilla. Top it with the bacon slices.

Over medium heat a non-stick skillet and pour in the eggs when the skillet is hot enough. As soon as the eggs begin to set, stir gently to form curds. Repeat mixing and folding the eggs until they are thickened and are in the right consistency.

Spoon the eggs over the bacon and fold the tortilla to cover the filling

Spray a different skillet with some non-stick spray and toast quesadillas giving them 1-2 minutes per side, until the cheese melts. Cut into serving portions then serve with your favorite salsa.

6. Anchovy-Egg Boats

A nice rich, creamy, salty, egg salad with quality anchovies served in crisp lettuce boats. A special dressing drizzled all over and topped with croutons for a great treat.

Serving Size: 3

Preparation Time: 8 minutes

Ingredients:

- ¼ cup store-bought croutons
- ½ tablespoon olive oil
- 3 hard-boiled eggs, peeled and sliced
- 1 gem lettuce, washed and torn into bite-sized pieces
- 2 tablespoons anchovy fillets, cut into 2 cm strips
- For the Dressing:
- 1 teaspoon crushed garlic
- 1 egg yolk
- 1 ½ teaspoons mustard
- 1 tablespoon lemon juice
- ¼ teaspoon sugar
- ½ cup extra virgin olive oil
- Salt and pepper to taste

Instructions:

For the dressing: In a suitable size bowl, combine all ingredients for the dressing except the olive oil. Pour the oil in a slow steady stream while whisking, to produce a smooth dressing.

Shell the hard-boiled eggs and cut into squares.

Arrange 2 pieces of lettuce in a serving platter, add the boiled eggs then top with croutons and sprinkle with dressing. Serve.

7. Eggs and Veggies Casserole

Eggs and Veggies Casserole, a sure crowd pleaser. This dish will wow your guests and it is easy to make, very tasty, packed with delicious ham slices and a variety of palatable cheeses. It is well seasoned with flavors we enjoy. This filling dish is very nutritious as it is complemented with a variety of vegetable additions.

Serving Size: 6

Preparation Time: 50 minutes

Ingredients:

- ¾ cup grated cheddar cheese
- 1 ¼ cups grated mozzarella cheese
- 1 tablespoon unsalted butter
- ½ cup sliced mushrooms (canned)
- ¼ cup thinly sliced red onions
- 3 tablespoons thinly chopped red bell pepper
- 1 cup cooked ham, diced
- 3 large eggs
- ¾ cup milk
- 2 tablespoons water
- ¼ cup all-purpose flour
- ¾ tablespoon minced parsley
- ¼ teaspoon dried basil
- ¼ teaspoon salt
- Pinch of black pepper

Instructions:

Preheat the oven to 350 degrees F.

Combine cheddar and mozzarella in a small bowl. In a 7x11 baking dish, place two-thirds of the cheese mixture at the bottom and spread evenly.

Over medium heat, in your saucepan melt the butter and sauté onions, mushrooms, bell pepper, until tender and cooked through. Drain the mixture and pour over the cheese mixture, spread evenly. Top with the diced ham and the remaining part of the cheese mixture.

Whisk together milk, water, flour, parsley, basil, pepper and salt in a small bowl. Pour into baking dish

Bake in a preheated oven for 30 to 40 minutes.

8. Egg in a Hole with Smoked Salmon

Dress up eggs in a hole with some smoked salmon. Share this with friends or family for brunch. The simple ingredients come together to make a scrumptious meal.

Serving Size: 2

Preparation Time: 10 minutes

Ingredients:

- 2 slices of country bread
- 2 large eggs
- 4 ounces smoked salmon
- ½ red onion, thinly sliced
- 1 tablespoon unsalted butter
- ¼ cup crème fraiche
- 1 tablespoon capers
- Black pepper to taste

Instructions:

Use a cookie cutter or a small glass to cut the center of the bread.

Melt butter in a skillet and place bread into a pot then break the egg into the center of the bread.

Cook for 1-2 minutes until the bread is golden. Flip over and cook until set on the other side.

Serve topped with salmon, capers, onion and crème. Add salt and pepper to taste.

9. Sausage and Cheese Omelet

Here is a classic omelet for you loaded with vitamins and minerals and a terrific blend of cheese, onions and sausage. This is great for you especially if you are in a hurry.

Serving Size: 2

Preparation Time: 10 minutes

Ingredients:

- 6 eggs
- 4 teaspoons unsalted butter
- 4 tablespoons cheddar cheese
- 1 breakfast sausage, removed from the casing and crumbled
- Salt and pepper to taste

Instructions:

Beat eggs, pepper and salt together.

Melt a little butter in a skillet (non-stick), spread it around and coat the pan. Pour half of the beaten eggs in; fry until set but the omelet must remain soft in the center.

In the center of the omelet lay half of the sausage and cheese, cook until the cheese has fully melted.

Fold omelet equally; remove from skillet and place it gently on a serving plate. Chopped green onions can be used for garnishing if you so desire. You can garnish some chopped green onions if you desire. Procedure should be repeated for another omelet.

10. Eggs Benedict

Eggs Benedict is a favorite Sunday breakfast, perfect to have a filling start to the day. Many people avoid making this, as they believe sauce hollandaise is difficult to prepare, but with this microwavable recipe, it's simple and yet delicious.

Serving Size: 2

Preparation Time: 20 minutes

Ingredients:

- 1 English breakfast muffin
- 2 large eggs
- 2 tablespoons white-wine vinegar
- 2 slices of ham
- 1/2 cup raw baby spinach
- 1 egg yolk
- 1 tablespoon mayonnaise
- 1 tablespoon fresh lemon juice
- 1/2 cup butter
- Salt
- Cayenne pepper

Instructions:

Fill a deep non-stick pan with water and add vinegar. Heat up until bubbles appear at the bottom of the pan, do not bring to a rolling boil.

Heat another pan and add ham to brown.

Melt your butter in the microwave. In another bowl, mix mayonnaise, lemon juice and egg yolk. While whisking, pour in your melted butter. Add one tbsp of water.

Crack your eggs into the boiling vinegar water and cook for 2 minutes (soft yolk) to 3 minutes (firm yolk). After, take them out with a scoop and place them on a plate with a paper towel.

While the egg is boiling, cut open your English muffin and toast the halves.

Place hollandaise into the microwave and microwave in 20 second bursts, whisking it between each burst until desired temperature. If the sauce curdles at the edges of the bowl, whisk thoroughly until it is smooth again and do not microwave it again.

Butter your muffin halves, add the spinach leaves, the ham and one egg each. Add salt and cayenne pepper to the hollandaise to taste. Pour sauce on each half, garnish with pepper and serve. Enjoy!

11. Eggs a La Goldenrod

A real soothing meal. With its warm toasty biscuits or puff pastry shells, topped with velvety hard-boiled eggs simmered in a special creamy warm sauce. What a great way to start your day!

Serving Size: 2

Preparation Time: 12 minutes

Ingredients:

- 3 hard-boiled eggs, peeled and chopped
- 1 tablespoon butter
- 1 ½ tablespoons all-purpose flour
- 1 cup milk
- 2 warm biscuits or frozen puff pastry shells, baked according to package instructions
- ½ tablespoon fresh parsley, chopped
- ⅛ teaspoon paprika powder
- Salt and pepper to taste

Instructions:

Over medium heat melt butter in your saucepan; stir in the flour and make a roux.

Cook roux until it is slightly golden for roughly 7 minutes. Pour in milk and stir 'til sauce thickens. Add salt and pepper to desired taste then stir in the chopped eggs.

Pour the egg mixture into biscuits / pastry shells to assemble, top it with parsley or paprika.

12. Mexican Egg and Potato Breakfast Skillet

This hearty egg dish may look like a lot but it is super quick. The bold flavors and textures will leave you wanting more.

Serving Size: 4

Preparation Time: 30 minutes

Ingredients:

- 1 tablespoon olive oil
- 4 eggs
- ¼ teaspoon salt
- ¼ cup salsa
- 1 tablespoon chopped cilantro
- 2 cups frozen potatoes
- ¼ cup milk
- Black pepper to taste
- ¼ cup tortilla chips
- ½ cup shredded Mexican cheese blend

Instructions:

Heat skillet then add oil and heat thoroughly. Put in potatoes and cook for 8 minutes until golden.

Combine milk, pepper, eggs and salt in a bowl and add to potatoes. Pull eggs across the skillet as they set and cook until firm.

Add cheese and take from the flame. Cover and put aside until the cheese has melted.

Top with cilantro, chips and salsa. Serve and enjoy!

13. Bell Pepper Baked Eggs

Impress your taste buds with these adorable Bell Pepper Baked Eggs, a delightful meal perfect for a charming breakfast or brunch experience. This quick and easy recipe is a cute and tasty twist on traditional eggs, making it an instant hit at your next breakfast gathering.

Serving Size: 4

Preparation Time: 23 minutes

Ingredients:

- 4 mini bell peppers, colors of choice
- 4 medium eggs
- Salt and black pepper
- Other seasonings of choice (qty. as desired)

Instructions:

Preheat your oven to 400 deg. F and line your baking sheet with greaseproof paper.

Slice off heads of bell peppers, deseed and remove membranes.

Arrange bell peppers on a baking sheet and crack an egg into each.

Place the baking sheet in the oven then bake for 16 to 18 minutes until bell peppers are tender, egg whites set and yolk still a bit runny.

Remove from the oven and season with salt, black pepper and other seasonings as desired.

Serve warm for breakfast.

14. Egg Drop Soup

If you are familiar with this dish from all the popular Chinese restaurants, then you will love the version that comes from your kitchen. Enjoy this comforting and flavorful soup that's sure to warm your heart and satisfy your taste buds.

Serving Size: 4

Preparation Time: 10 minutes

Ingredients:

- 2 tablespoons cornstarch
- 3 tablespoons water
- 14 ounces chicken broth
- 1 cup water
- ½ tomato, diced
- ¼ teaspoon white pepper
- ¼ teaspoon salt
- 2 eggs, beaten lightly

Instructions:

Mix cornstarch with 3 tablespoons of water and put aside till needed.

Heat broth and 1 cup water then add salt, pepper, and tomato.

Add a little cornstarch to thicken; stir and remove from flame.

Swirl eggs into soup then stir right away with chopsticks.

Cover for 2 minutes.

When eggs are set, serve and enjoy.

15. Avgolemono Soup

Indulge in the refreshing and delightful taste of Greek Avgolemono Soup, a zesty lemon-infused chicken broth enriched with tender shredded chicken and hearty rice. This satisfying soup is simmered to perfection with aromatic herbs and vegetables, delivering a burst of flavors in every spoonful.

Serving Size: 8

Preparation Time: 2 hours and 25 minutes

Ingredients:

- 1 (about 4 pounds) whole chicken
- 8 cups water
- Salt and pepper to taste
- ½ cup chopped celery
- 2 peeled and sliced carrots
- 1 bay leaf
- Dash of oregano
- Dash of thyme
- 1 tablespoon olive oil
- 1 diced onion
- ¾ cup short-grain rice
- 2 eggs
- ¼ cup fresh lemon juice

Instructions:

Place the chicken in a soup pot and cover with water.

Season with salt and pepper.

Add the celery, carrots, bay leaf, oregano and thyme.

Stir all the ingredients and cover the pot.

Simmer for 1 hour and 30 minutes.

Transfer the chicken to a platter.

Strain the broth and discard all vegetables.

Heat the olive oil in your skillet then sauté the onion for 5 minutes.

Stir the onions into the broth.

10. Add the rice and adjust the seasoning.

Cover the pot and simmer for 50 minutes.

Whisk the eggs and lemon juice together then combine with a cup of broth from the pot.

Drizzle the lemon/broth into the soup while stirring.

Shred the chicken and transfer the meat back to the pot. 15. Simmer for an additional 5 minutes.

16. Egg Soufflé

An Egg Soufflé casserole is the favorite thing of French cooks to do with eggs. It is a light and flavorful dish that is usually served for brunch, especially on special occasions.

Serving Size: 6

Preparation Time: 1 hour and 15 minutes

Ingredients:

- 10 pcs eggs, yolks and whites separated
- 3.5 ounces goat cheese, crumbled
- ¼ cup fresh dill, chopped
- 1 garlic clove, minced
- 1 teaspoon fresh lemon juice
- 4 tablespoons unsalted butter
- 2 ¼ cups whole milk
- 4 tablespoons all-purpose flour
- ¾ teaspoon salt
- Freshly ground black pepper to taste
- Cooking spray

Instructions:

Preheat the oven to 350 deg. F. Prepare a baking tray lightly greased with cooking spray.

Meanwhile, melt butter in a pan on medium fire and sprinkle flour. Stir for about 1 minute.

Gradually add milk and simmer until thick.

Stir in garlic, cheese, salt, and pepper. Let it simmer for a few minutes, then turn off the heat and let it cool.

Whisk together egg yolks and dill in a large bowl. Set aside.

Whisk the egg whites and lemon juice using an electric mixer until stiff.

Fold the egg white mixture into the yolk's mixture until well incorporated.

Transfer to your prepared pan, bake for about 30 minutes, placing at the lower third of the oven so the top does not burn.

Serve and enjoy.

17. Spinach, Ham and Cheese Omelet

This quick omelet is full of protein as well as Vitamin D. The spinach, ham and cheese make a filling start to the day.

Serving Size: 1

Preparation Time: 10 minutes

Ingredients:

- 2 eggs
- 1 teaspoon butter
- ¼ cup shredded Italian cheese blend
- ¼ cup diced ham
- 2 tablespoons water
- Salt to taste
- ¼ cup baby spinach
- Black pepper to taste

Instructions:

Put eggs and water in a bowl and beat to combine.

Melt butter in a skillet and coat pan then add eggs.

As edges set, push to the middle and cook until the rest of the eggs set. Push more of the cooked parts into the center if necessary.

Use salt and pepper to season egg and top with spinach, ham and cheese. Fold and remove from the pan.

Serve and enjoy!

18. Avocado Eggs

Here is another witty idea to enjoy eggs. This is basically just like the egg cups. Instead of muffin tins, however, the eggs are cracked into avocado halves to make it a lot healthier and exciting. With the additional creaminess of the avocado meat, the dish gets a new layer of texture that will make your mealtime even more interesting. Plus, this dish is loaded with choline and vitamin A, among many other nutrients.

Serving Size: 4

Preparation Time: 15 minutes

Ingredients:

- 4 pcs eggs
- 2 pcs ripe avocados, halved and pitted
- ¼ cup fresh parsley, chopped
- 2 tablespoons olive oil
- Salt and freshly ground pepper to taste

Instructions:

Preheat the oven to 375 deg. F. Prepare your baking sheet lined with aluminum foil.

Arrange the avocado halves into the baking sheet, making sure it remains upright. You may scoop out some meat to ensure that the hole can hold a full egg. Brush the avocado meat with some olive oil.

Crack the eggs carefully into each of the avocado halves, sprinkle with a pinch of salt and pepper to taste.

Place the baking sheet into the oven and cook for about 15 minutes or until the eggs are set.

Garnish with freshly chopped parsley and serve.

19. Bacon and Cheddar Deviled Eggs

These cheesy deviled eggs are complete with the addition of bacon. Bring these to the next potluck or family brunch.

Serving Size: 24

Preparation Time: 30 minutes

Ingredients:

- 14 hard-boiled eggs
- ½ cup sour cream
- 1 teaspoon lemon juice
- 1/3 cup cooked and crumbled bacon
- 2 tablespoons chives
- ½ cup mayonnaise
- 1 ½ teaspoons Dijon mustard
- ¼ teaspoon black pepper
- ¼ cup shredded cheddar cheese

Instructions:

Slice eggs in half and take out yolks. Put 24 halves aside and chop remaining whites.

Crush yolks and add sour cream, lemon juice, pepper and mayonnaise. Combine then add bacon, chives, whites and cheese.

Spoon mixture into reserved egg whites.

Cover and refrigerate before serving.

20. Huevos Rancheros

Exotic, fried ranch-style eggs. These are served on tortillas and can be served with some chilies, salsa, peppers, tomatoes, and a variety of different savory Mexican toppings.

Serving Size: 4

Preparation Time: 30 minutes

Ingredients:

- 1 teaspoon olive oil
- ½ cup onion, chopped
- 2 large tomatoes, diced
- 5 tablespoons diced green chilies
- 4 corn tortillas
- 4 large eggs
- 1 tablespoon fresh cilantro, chopped
- 2 tablespoons butter
- Salt and pepper to taste

Instructions:

Prepare sauce by sautéing the onions in the olive oil, over medium heat in your non-stick skillet. Add tomatoes and the green chilies and cook until all tomatoes are broken down. Lower the heat and let sauce simmer for ten minutes. Turn off the heat Season well with salt and pepper.

Over medium high heat, in a large non-stick skillet, heat the tortillas 2 minutes per side. Set aside.

In the same skillet, melt the butter then pan fry the eggs for 4 minutes.

To assemble, pour some sauce into a serving plate then top with tortilla and fried egg. Top with cilantro. Do the same for the other tortillas. Serve.

21. Broccoli and Cheddar Omelet

This omelet can be made for breakfast or lunch. Crunchy broccoli is a great addition to these eggs. Pair this omelet with a fruit salad and more fillings if you please.

Serving Size: 1

Preparation Time: 7 minutes

Ingredients:

- 2 eggs
- 1/3 cup cooked broccoli florets
- Salt to taste
- 2 tablespoons water
- 2 tablespoons shredded cheddar cheese
- Black pepper to taste

Instructions:

Put eggs and water in a bowl and beat to combine.

Heat the skillet and use cooking spray to coat the pan. Add eggs to your pan and allow to cook.

As edges set, push to the middle and cook until the rest of the eggs set. Push more of the cooked parts into the center if necessary.

Use salt and pepper to season the egg and top with broccoli and cheese. Fold and remove from the pan.

Serve and enjoy!

22. Egg and Sausage Casserole

Packed with flavorful sweet Italian sausages, vibrant spinach, and oil-packed sun-dried tomatoes, this casserole is a delight for your taste buds. Baked to perfection with a luscious blend of eggs and cheddar cheese, this warm and satisfying casserole is perfect for a cozy breakfast or brunch with loved ones, making your mornings even more delightful.

Serving Size: 4

Preparation Time: 1 hour and 5 minutes

Ingredients:

- 2 tablespoons olive oil + extra for greasing
- ½ pound bread, cut into 1-inch cubes
- ½ pound sweet Italian sausages, casings removed
- 1 medium onion, finely chopped
- 1 cup spinach
- 1/3 cup oil-packed sun-dried tomatoes, nicely drained and chopped
- 12 large eggs
- ½ cup whole milk
- Salt and black pepper to taste
- ¼ cup grated cheddar cheese

Instructions:

Preheat your oven to 400 F. With olive oil, grease a baking dish. Then, set aside.

On a large baking sheet, toss bread with 1 tablespoon of olive oil then spread on the bottom of the baking dish. Bake in the oven for 10 minutes.

Meanwhile, heat remaining olive oil in your medium skillet over medium heat.

Add sausages and onion; cook and crumble for 8 to 10 minutes or until golden brown.

Stir in sun-dried tomatoes, turn heat off and stir in spinach. Set aside.

Crack eggs into your large bowl, add milk, salt, black pepper, and whisk smoothly.

Toss in bread, sausage mixture and mix well.

Spread mixture in baking dish and scatter cheddar cheese on top.

Bake for 40 to 45 minutes or until the cheese melts, is golden brown and the casserole is just set in the center.

Remove the baking dish and serve warm.

23. Shakshuka (Eggs in Tomato Sauce)

Shakshuka is an egg dish that originated from the Middle East. It is also a popular dish in Mediterranean cuisine. It is basically poached eggs that are cooked in a delightful tomato-based sauce with a few other ingredients that include bell peppers and cheese, among others. Shakshuka is often served with some crusty bread or rice, good for lunch or dinner.

Serving Size: 4

Preparation Time: 25 minutes

Ingredients:

- 6 pcs eggs
- 1 pc red bell pepper, thinly sliced
- 1 pc yellow onion, thinly sliced
- 1 (15-ounce) can white beans, drained & rinsed
- 1 (28-ounce) can diced tomatoes
- ½ cup cilantro leaves, chopped
- ½ cup feta cheese, crumbled
- 2 tablespoons olive oil
- 1 teaspoon fennel seeds
- 1 teaspoon coriander seeds
- 1 teaspoon cumin seeds
- 1 teaspoon smoked paprika
- 1 teaspoon kosher salt
- Freshly ground black pepper to taste

Instructions:

Heat a cast iron skillet on medium fire and dry roast the fennel, coriander, and cumin seeds until fragrant. Let it cool down, then, transfer to a spice grinder and pulse until powdered. Set aside.

Wipe your skillet with some paper towel and then, heat oil on medium high.

Sauté the onions and bell peppers until soft, about 10 minutes, stirring occasionally.

Sprinkle ground spices, plus paprika, and salt.

Gently add the tomatoes with its juices, and simmer for a few minutes.

Add the beans and cheese. Let it boil, then turn the heat to low and cook for about 5 minutes in a gentle simmer.

Make holes for the eggs and crack them one by one, sprinkle with salt and pepper, cover, and continue to cook on low for about 5 minutes more or until the eggs are completely set.

Garnish with freshly chopped cilantro and serve.

24. Egg Quiche Tarts

These little quiche tarts are extremely light and flaky. They are flavored with our all-time favorite and can be made ahead of time if preferred. A tasty brunch and is perfect with hot milk or coffee.

Serving Size: 5

Preparation Time: 30 minutes

Ingredients:

- ½ cup cream cheese, room temperature
- 2 tablespoons milk
- 1 large egg
- 2 tablespoons Swiss cheese, shredded
- 2 tablespoons cheddar cheese, shredded
- ½ cup and 2 tablespoons flaky biscuit dough, store-bought

Instructions:

Heat your oven to 375 degrees Fahrenheit. Grease 5 muffin cups and set aside.

In your mixing bowl, beat the eggs, cream cheese and milk until smooth. Stir in the Swiss and cheddar cheese then set aside.

Separate the dough into 5 biscuits then press each biscuit into the bottom and sides of each muffin mold.

In each greased mold, pour in about 2 tablespoons of the egg mixture.

Bake for 20 minutes or until the filing is set and the dough is nicely browned. Serve.

25. Poached Eggs on Avocado Toasts

Create a delightful snack in minutes with these Poached Eggs on Avocado Toasts, where perfectly poached eggs rest gracefully atop creamy mashed avocado seasoned with salt and black pepper. A delectable combination of flavors awaits you as you spread the avocado on toasted bread and crown it with the tender poached eggs, making this dish a quick and satisfying treat to savor anytime.

Serving Size: 2

Preparation Time: 11 minutes

Ingredients:

- 1 ripe avocado, pitted and peeled
- Salt and black pepper to taste
- 2 eggs
- 2 tablespoons plain vinegar
- 2 bread slices, toasted

Instructions:

Mash avocado in a bowl, season with salt, black pepper and set aside.

Bring your medium pot of water to a boil and then reduce heat to low.

Add vinegar and stir water in a circular motion to form a vortex.

Crack one egg into the center of the vortex and cook for 3 minutes or until egg white sets and yolk is runny.

Remove egg onto a paper towel-lined plate and cook the second egg the same way.

Spread avocado on bread and place a poached egg on each.

26. Egg and Sausage Burritos

Start your day with a burst of flavor and convenience with these Egg and Sausage Burritos, the perfect breakfast option whether enjoyed at home or on the go. Wrapped in warm flour tortillas, these burritos are a satisfying treat that will energize you for a productive day ahead.

Serving Size: 4

Preparation Time: 16 minutes

Ingredients:

- 2 tablespoons butter, divided
- 8 links breakfast sausages, casings removed and crumbled
- 1 medium yellow onion, chopped
- 1 medium red bell pepper, deseeded and chopped
- Salt and black pepper to taste
- 8 large eggs, lightly beaten
- 1 cup Monterey Jack cheese, grated
- 8 large flour tortillas or gluten-free tortillas

Instructions:

Melt 1 tablespoon of butter in your medium skillet over medium heat.

Add sausages; cook and crumble for 5 minutes or until golden brown. Transfer sausage to your plate then set aside.

Add onion and bell pepper to the skillet. Then, sauté for 3 minutes or until tender. Spoon vegetables to the side of sausages.

Clean skillet and melt in remaining butter over medium heat.

Pour in eggs and immediately scramble for 1 to 2 minutes or until set. Season with salt and black pepper.

Stir in cheese and let melt for 1 minute. Turn heat off.

Divide eggs onto tortillas, add sausages, vegetables and wrap up burritos.

Serve immediately.

27. Ham and Cheese Egg Cups

Making egg cups is another way to enjoy a protein-packed meal in the morning, deliciously served with coffee. You can make this particular recipe in about 20 minutes, so you will have lots more time to savor it, even during super busy days. It's great to have a delish breakfast to start the day. You will have more energy to keep up with the rest of your tasks ahead.

Serving Size: 4

Preparation Time: 17 minutes

Ingredients:

- 12 pcs eggs
- 12 pcs deli ham slices
- 1 cup Gruyere cheese, grated
- 1 tablespoon parsley, chopped
- Salt and pepper to taste
- Cooking spray

Instructions:

Preheat the oven to 400 deg. F. Prepare a 12-piece muffin tin lightly greased with some cooking spray.

Carefully arrange a piece of ham slice into each muffin tin, pressing to make a cup shape.

Place about a tablespoon of cheese on each muffin tin, then crack an egg. Repeat with the rest of the muffin tins.

Sprinkle top with salt and freshly ground pepper and bake for about 12 minutes or until the eggs are set.

To serve, gently lift the egg cups from the muffin tins, sprinkle with chopped parsley, plus more salt and pepper.

28. Mushroom and Ricotta Frittata

We love how ricotta cheese and mushrooms sit well in this frittata. You can serve it for breakfast, brunch, or even dinner.

Serving Size: 4

Preparation Time: 28 minutes

Ingredients:

- 8 large eggs
- 2 tablespoons olive oil
- ¼ cup Parmesan cheese, grated
- ½ cup part-skim ricotta cheese
- 2 leeks
- ½ cup sliced cremini mushrooms
- Salt and black pepper to taste

Instructions:

Heat oven to 400 F.

Crack eggs into your large bowl and whisk with Parmesan and ricotta cheeses. Set aside.

Over medium heat, heat olive oil in your ovenproof skillet.

Add leeks and mushrooms; sauté for 5 minutes or until tender. Season with salt and black pepper.

Pour on egg mixture and stir to distribute evenly.

Transfer pan skillet to oven then bake for 16 to 18 minutes or until eggs set.

Serve frittata warm.

29. Mexican Egg Scramble

Say goodbye to boring scrambled eggs and say hello to the delightful flavors of this Mexican Egg Scramble. With a touch of butter, well-beaten eggs and canned black beans come together in a scrumptious dance of taste. Elevate your breakfast experience with the richness of melted cheddar cheese, adding a comforting layer of gooey goodness to each bite.

Serving Size: 2

Preparation Time: 4 minutes

Ingredients:

- 1 teaspoon butter
- 2 eggs, well-beaten
- ¼ cup canned black beans, nicely drained and rinsed
- ¼ cup grated cheddar cheese
- 2 tablespoons salsa

Instructions:

Melt butter in your small skillet over medium heat.

Pour in eggs and beans. Immediately scramble for 1 minute.

Season with salt, black pepper and add cheddar cheese. Stir and cook for 1 minute or 'til cheese melts.

Spoon eggs onto a plate, top with salsa and serve warm.

30. Turmeric Egg Curry

Want to enjoy something vegetarian that is not short of protein content? Try this egg curry made more delicious by the flavors of turmeric and a delicious blend of spices that's widely used in Sri Lankan cuisine. This can be eaten with rice or flatbreads and is as satisfying either way.

Serving Size: 4

Preparation Time: 25 minutes

Ingredients:

- 8 pcs eggs, soft-boiled
- ¾ cup fresh curry leaves, divided
- 2 tablespoons ginger, finely chopped
- 1 pc onion, thinly sliced
- 4 cloves garlic, finely chopped
- 2 pcs long green chilies, thinly sliced
- 2 pcs pandan leaves, tied in a knot
- 1 (28-ounce) can coconut milk
- 2 tablespoons vegetable oil
- 1 teaspoon turmeric powder
- 1 pc cinnamon quill, broken into several pieces
- 1 teaspoon nigella seeds
- 1 tablespoon coriander seeds
- 1 teaspoon cumin seeds
- ½ teaspoon fenugreek
- 2 teaspoons fennel seeds
- 1 teaspoon salt flakes
- 1 teaspoon white peppercorns

Instructions:

In your mortar and pestle or a spice grinder, place turmeric, ¼ cup of curry leaves, nigella seeds, cinnamon, fenugreek, cumin, fennel, salt flakes, and peppercorns. Process until the spices are finely ground. Set aside.

Meanwhile, heat oil in your pan on medium fire and sauté the ginger, onion, garlic, curry leaves, and chili until fragrant, about 5 minutes, stirring occasionally.

Stir in prepared spice mix with turmeric and cook for another 2 minutes.

Pour in coconut milk, plus water, eggs, and pandan leaves. Boil, then, turn heat to low, and simmer for about 15 minutes or until the sauce is thickened.

Serve with hot steamed rice and enjoy.

Conclusion

In conclusion, this book has unveiled the vast potential of eggs beyond the usual scrambled preparation. As you've explored various cooking methods and recipes, you've likely gained a deeper appreciation for the versatility of eggs in enhancing texture, flavor, and nutritional value in your dishes. Perhaps you've discovered new ways to delight your kids with eggs, transforming their once-disliked ingredient into a favorite meal, or you've learned how to create healthier and more nutritious family breakfasts.

Armed with this newfound knowledge, you are now equipped to embark on culinary experimentation, exploring exciting ways to modify classic recipes or elevate your meals with the addition of this incredible ingredient. Don't hesitate to venture into the realm of unique egg varieties like duck or quail eggs, which offer surprisingly delightful tastes and textures.

In the end, your culinary journey with eggs has just begun, and there are countless avenues to explore. Embrace the endless possibilities and enjoy the satisfaction of creating scrumptious egg-based dishes that will surely leave you and your loved ones craving for more. Bon appétit!

Wish You the Best

thank you

I am deeply grateful for your decision to download and read this book. It's my pleasure to share the knowledge and skills I've acquired, along with valuable tips, through the magic of writing. I trust that your experience has been both enjoyable and educational.

In a world brimming with books, I appreciate the time and thought you put into selecting mine. Your choice speaks volumes, and I'm confident that you found it to be a rewarding read.

Your honest feedback would bring me immense joy. Constructive critiques have been instrumental in my growth as an author and continue to influence my work. Your insights help me refine my content and inspire new ideas, potentially sparking the concept for my next book.

Once again, thank you for embarking on this literary journey with me.

Joris Birt

Printed in Great Britain
by Amazon